This Journal Belongs To:

DOUBLE DANCE DESIGNS

Made in United States
North Haven, CT
02 May 2025

68523171R00072